You Are Bullshit

A Vulgar Words

Adult Coloring Book for Release Anger

By

S.B. Nozaz

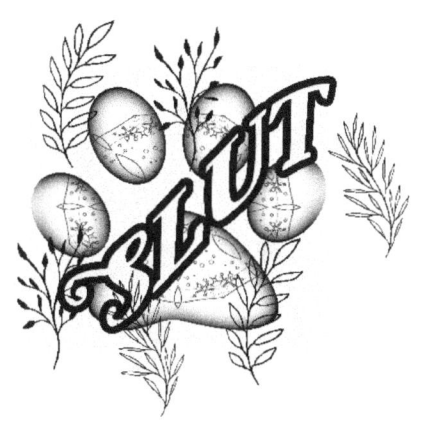

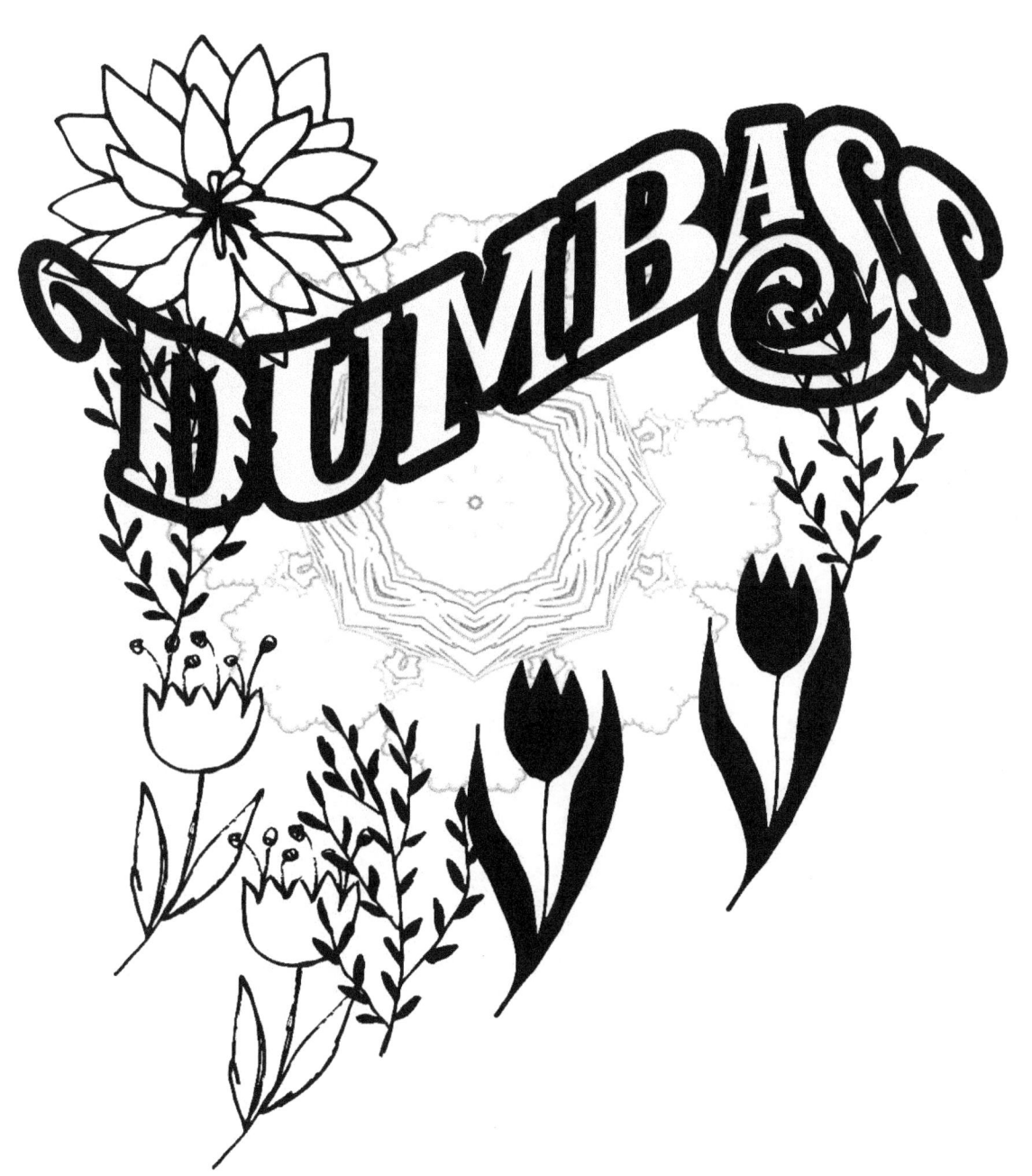

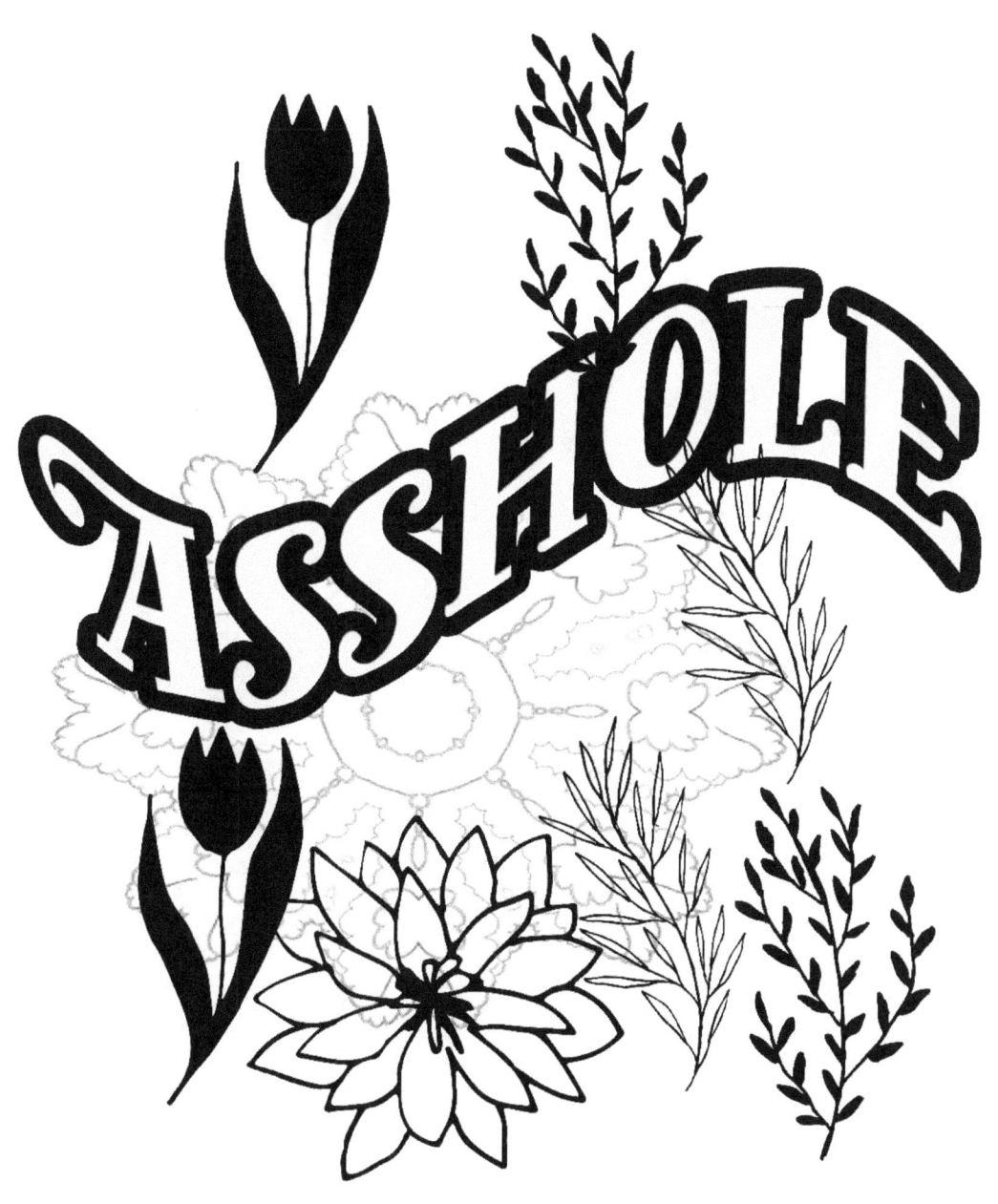

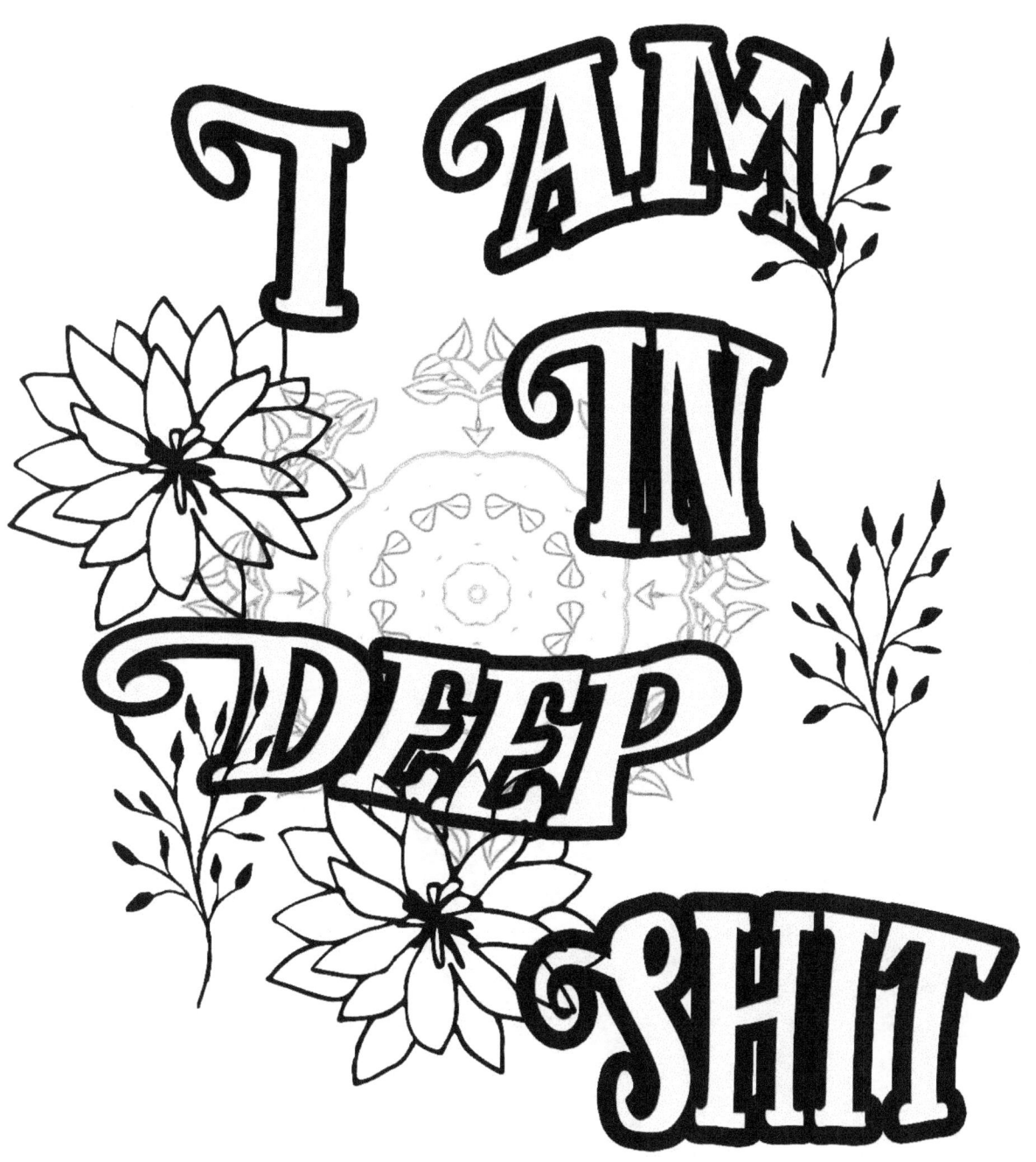

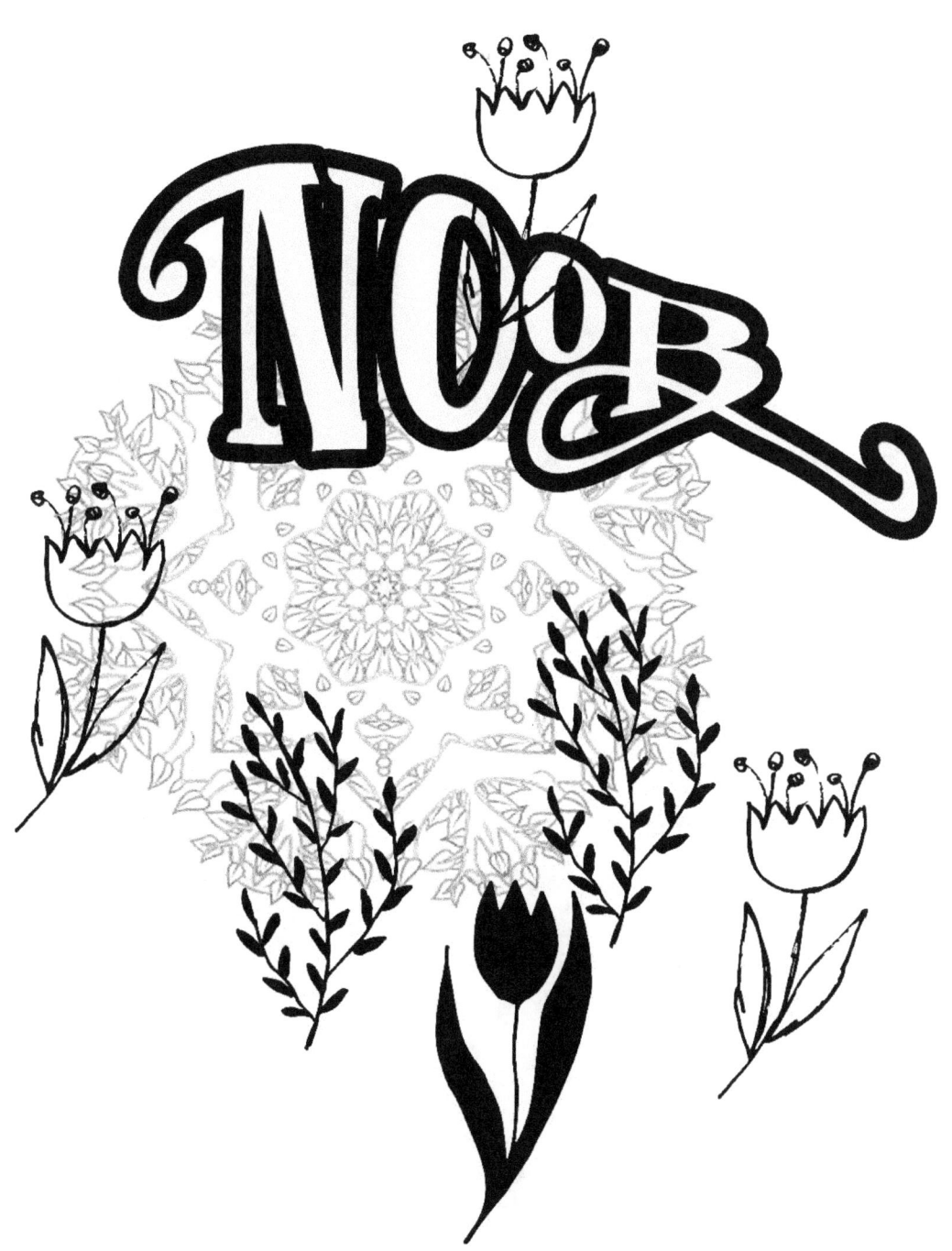

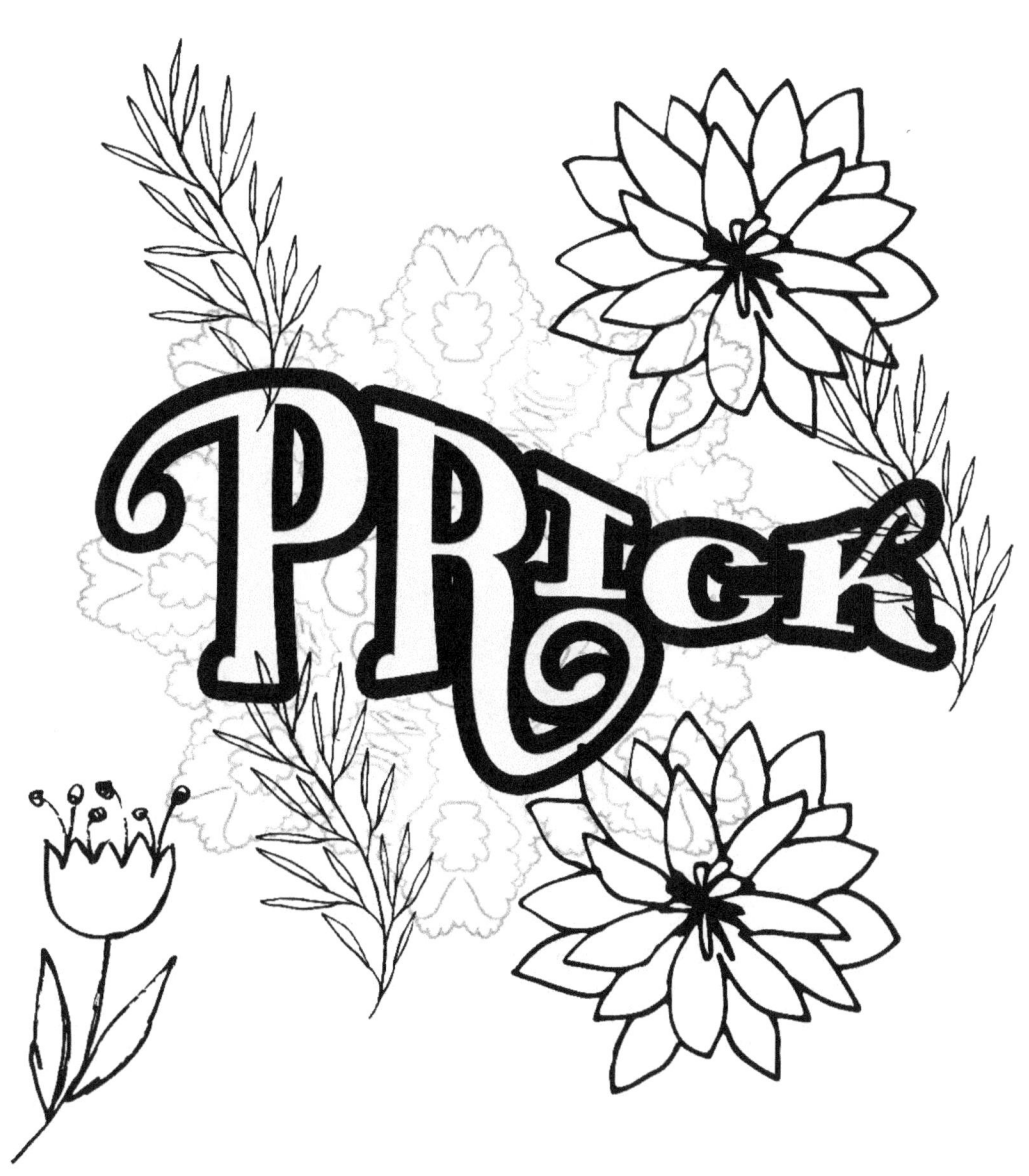

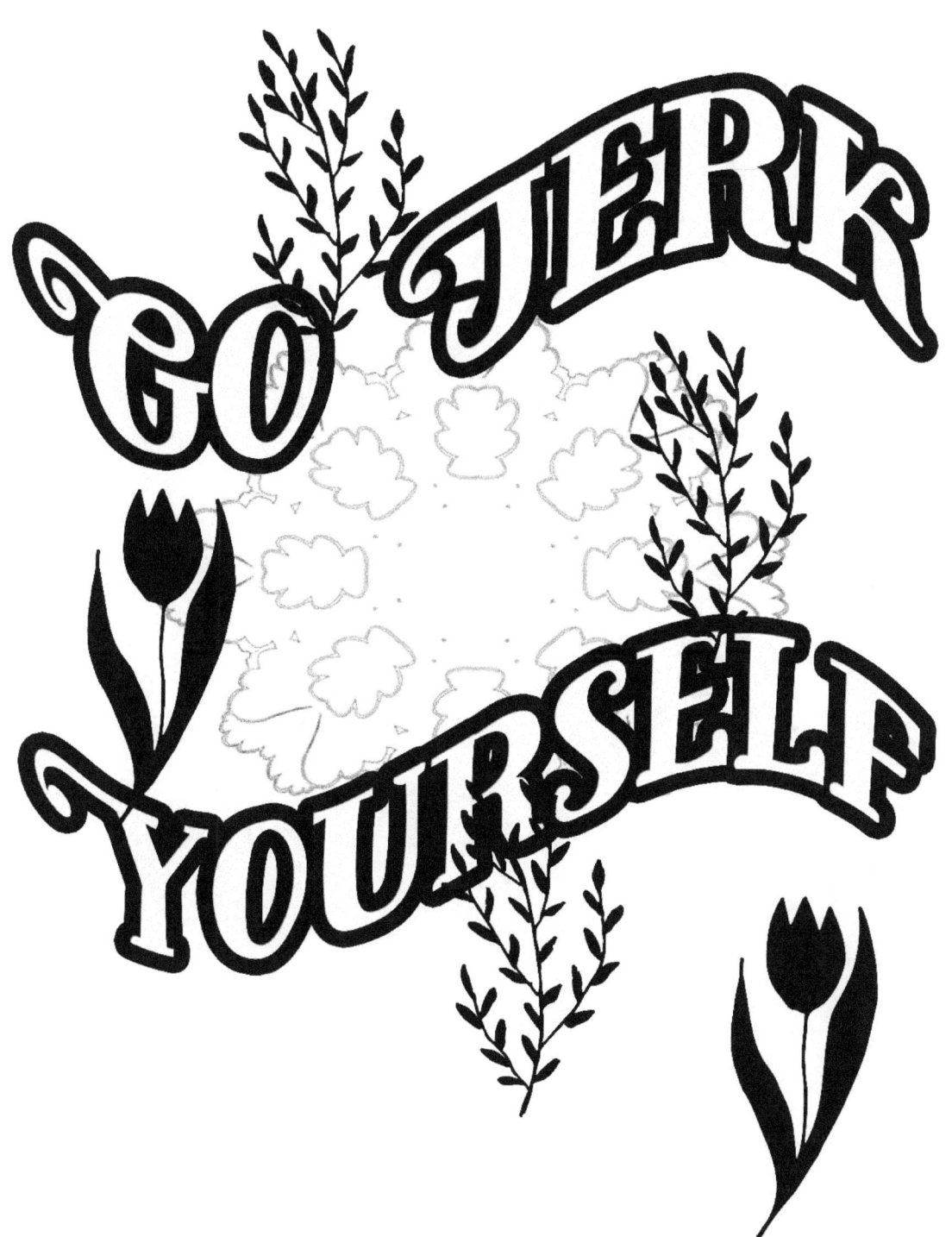

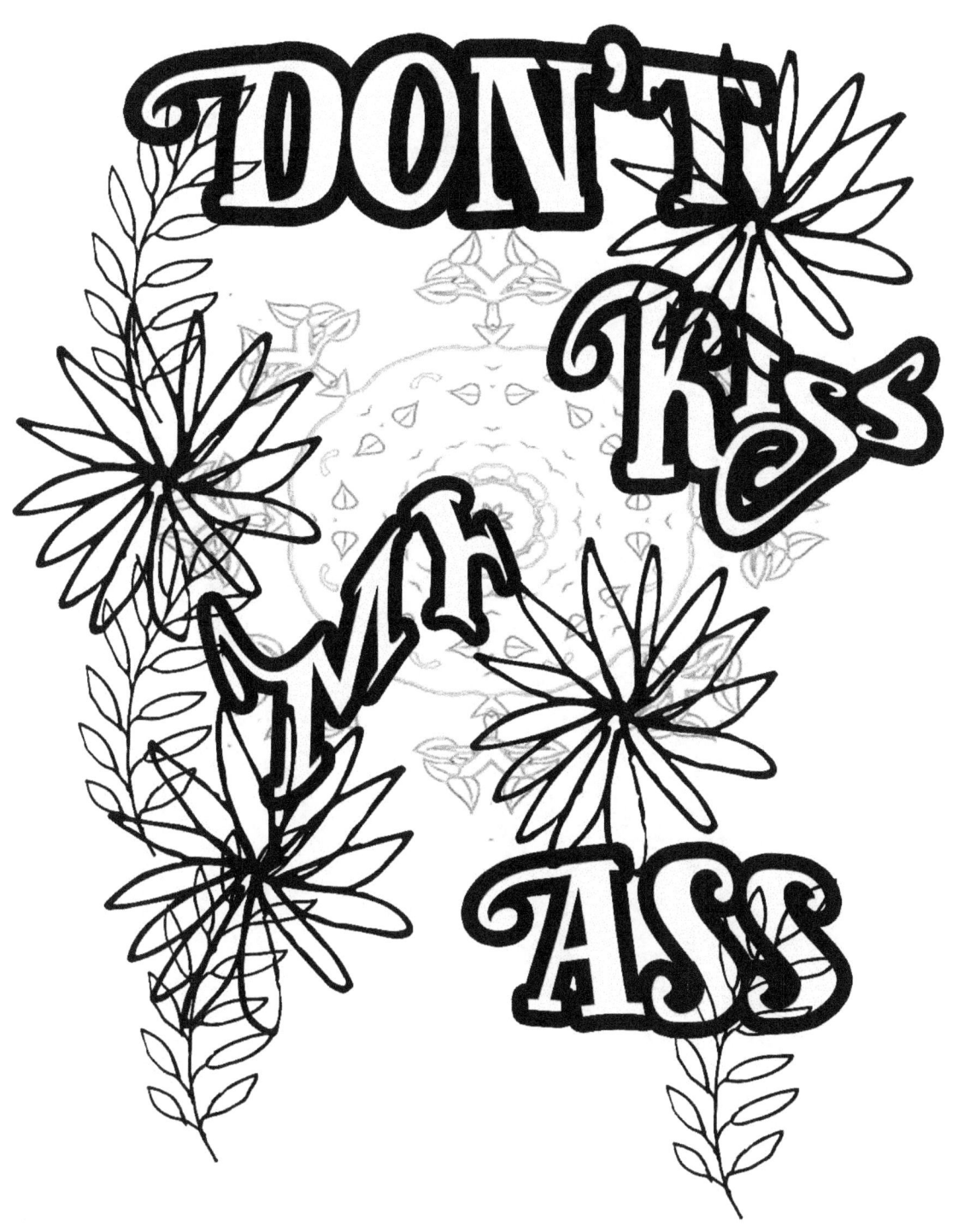

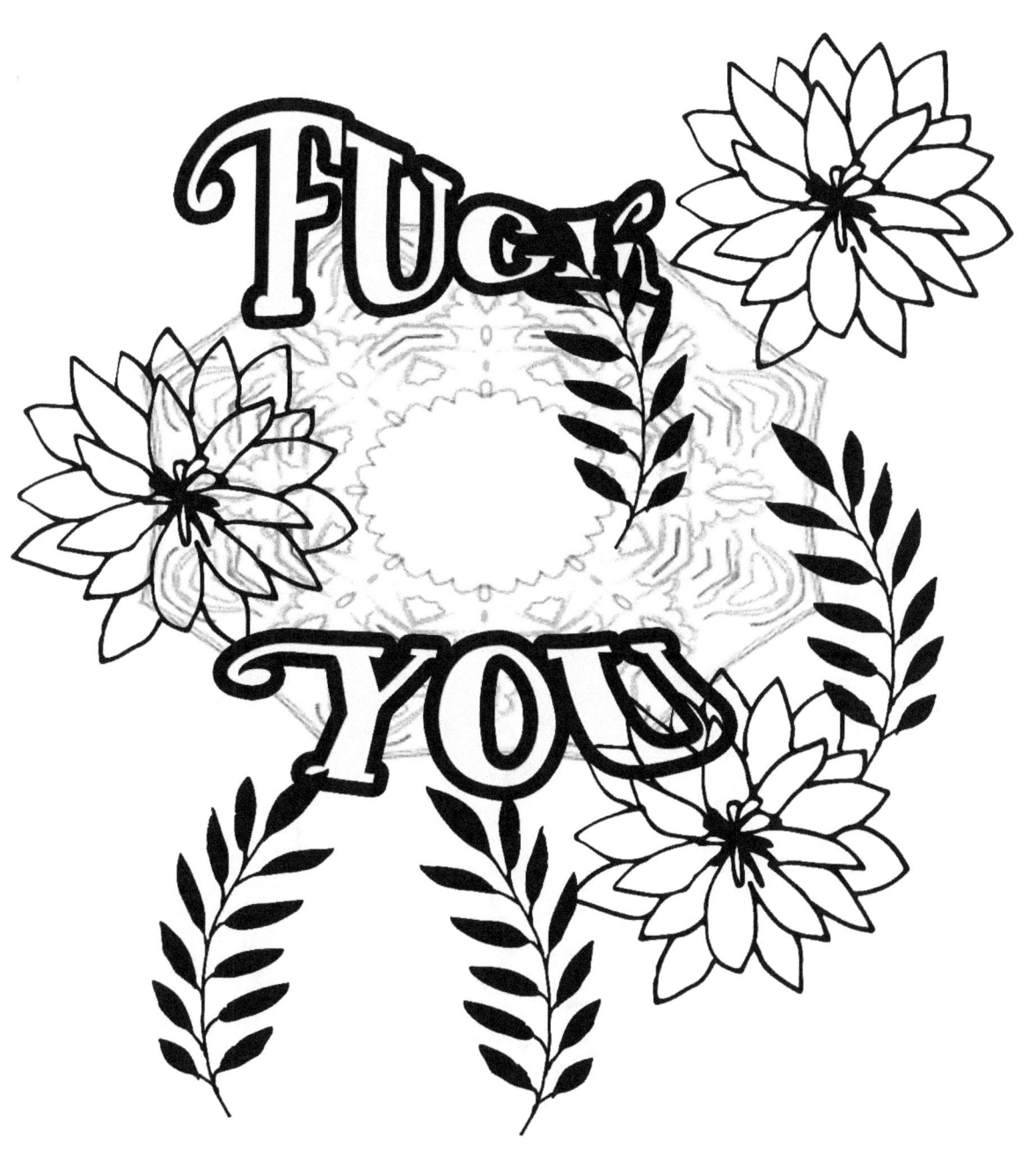

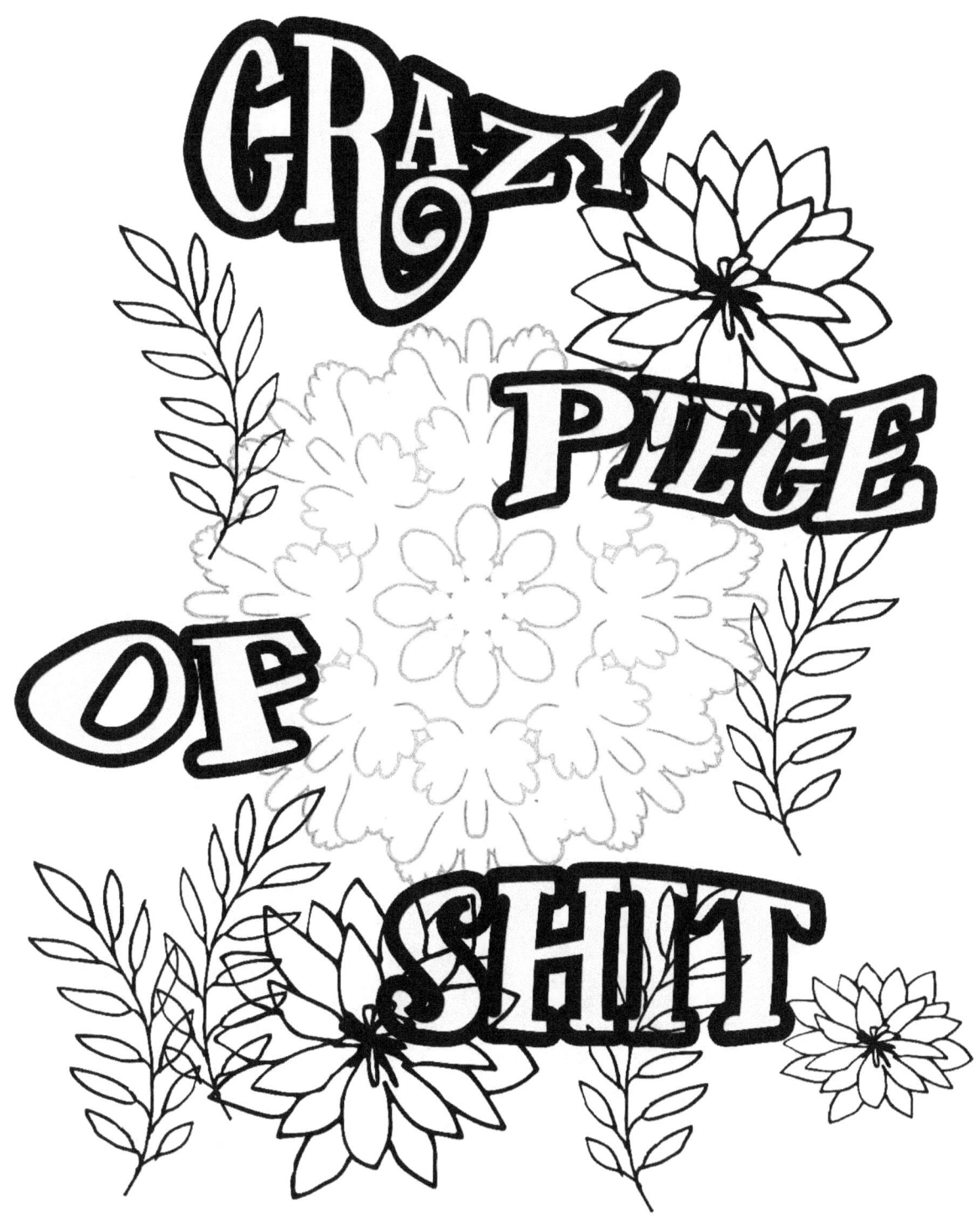

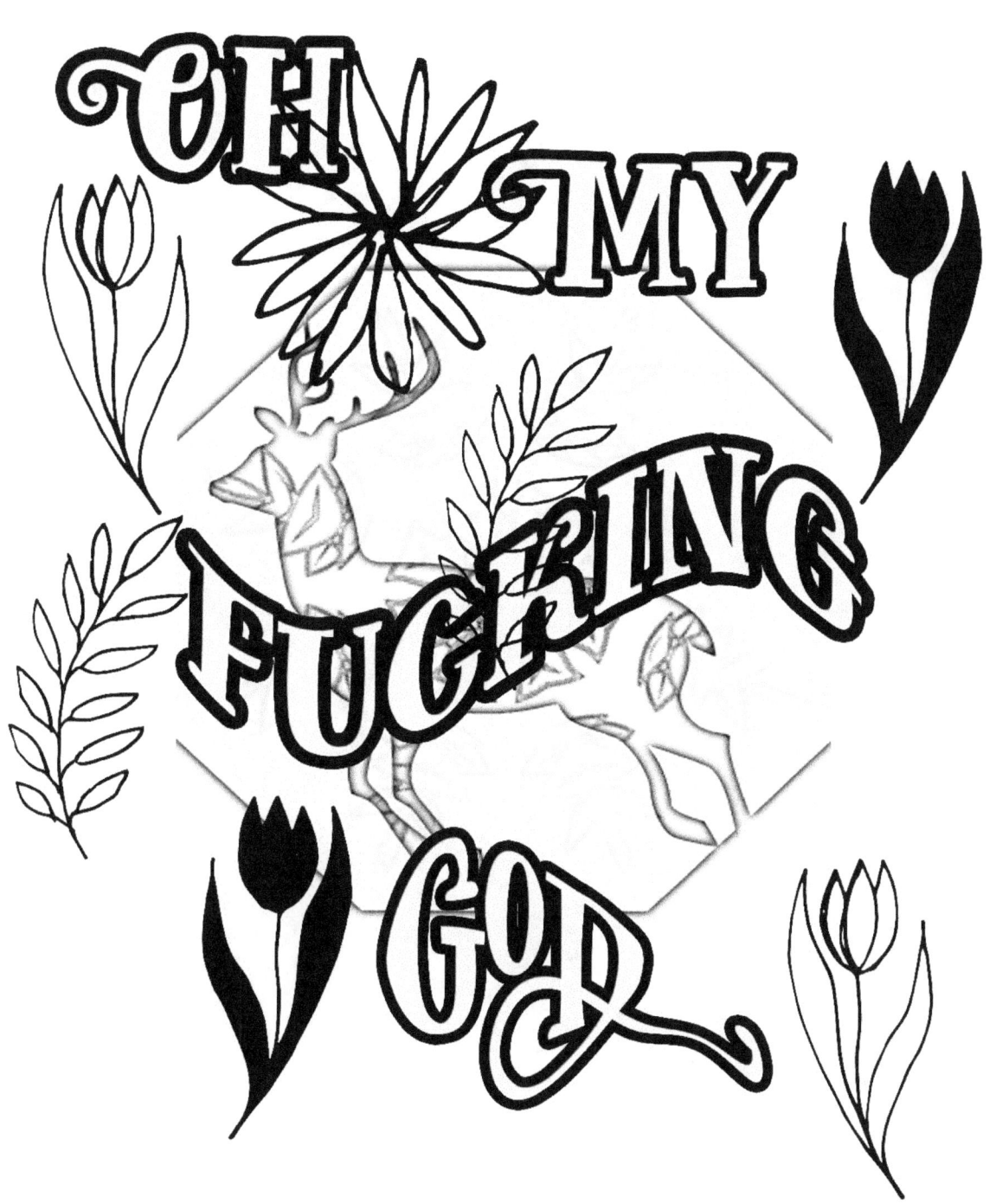

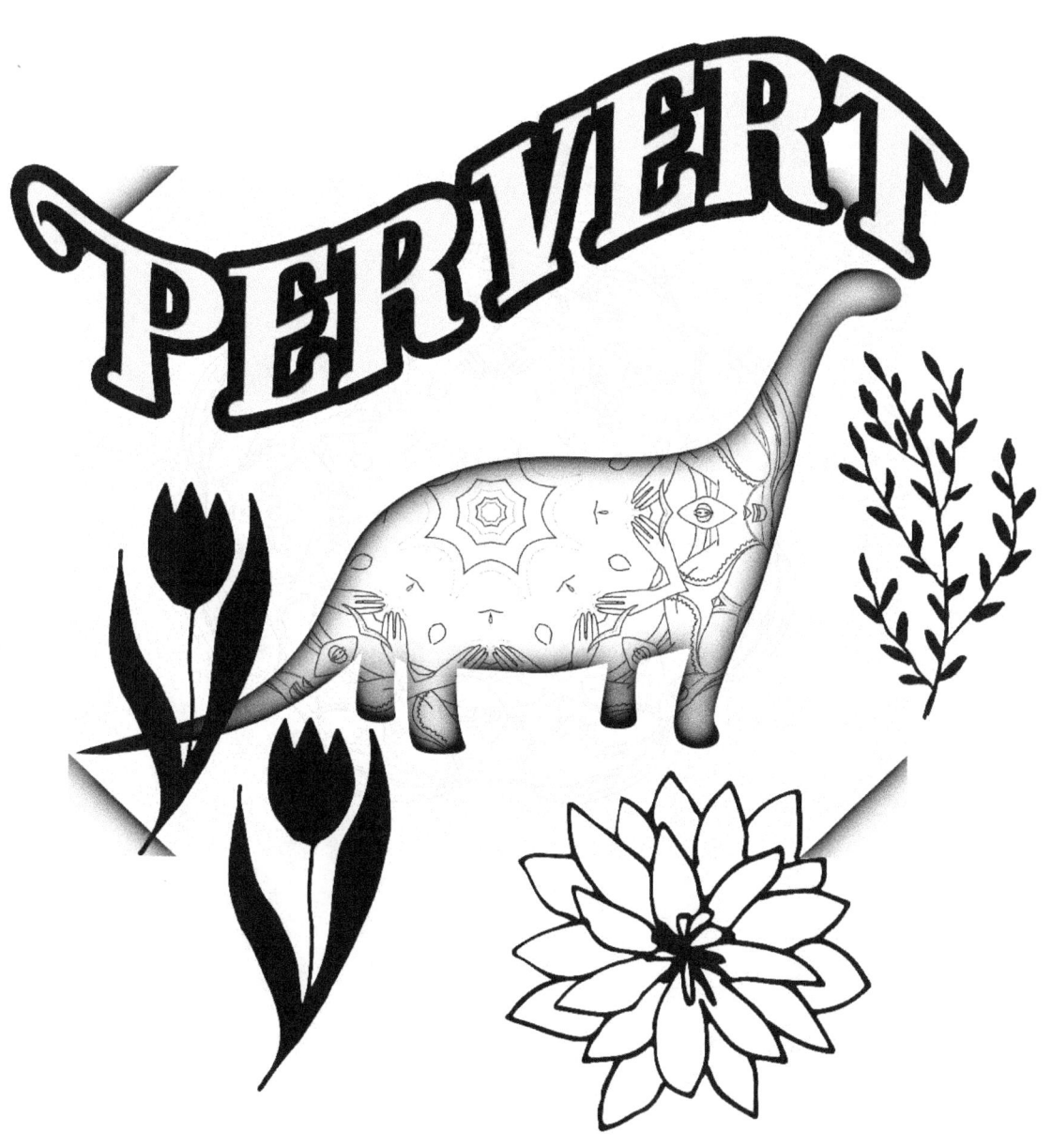

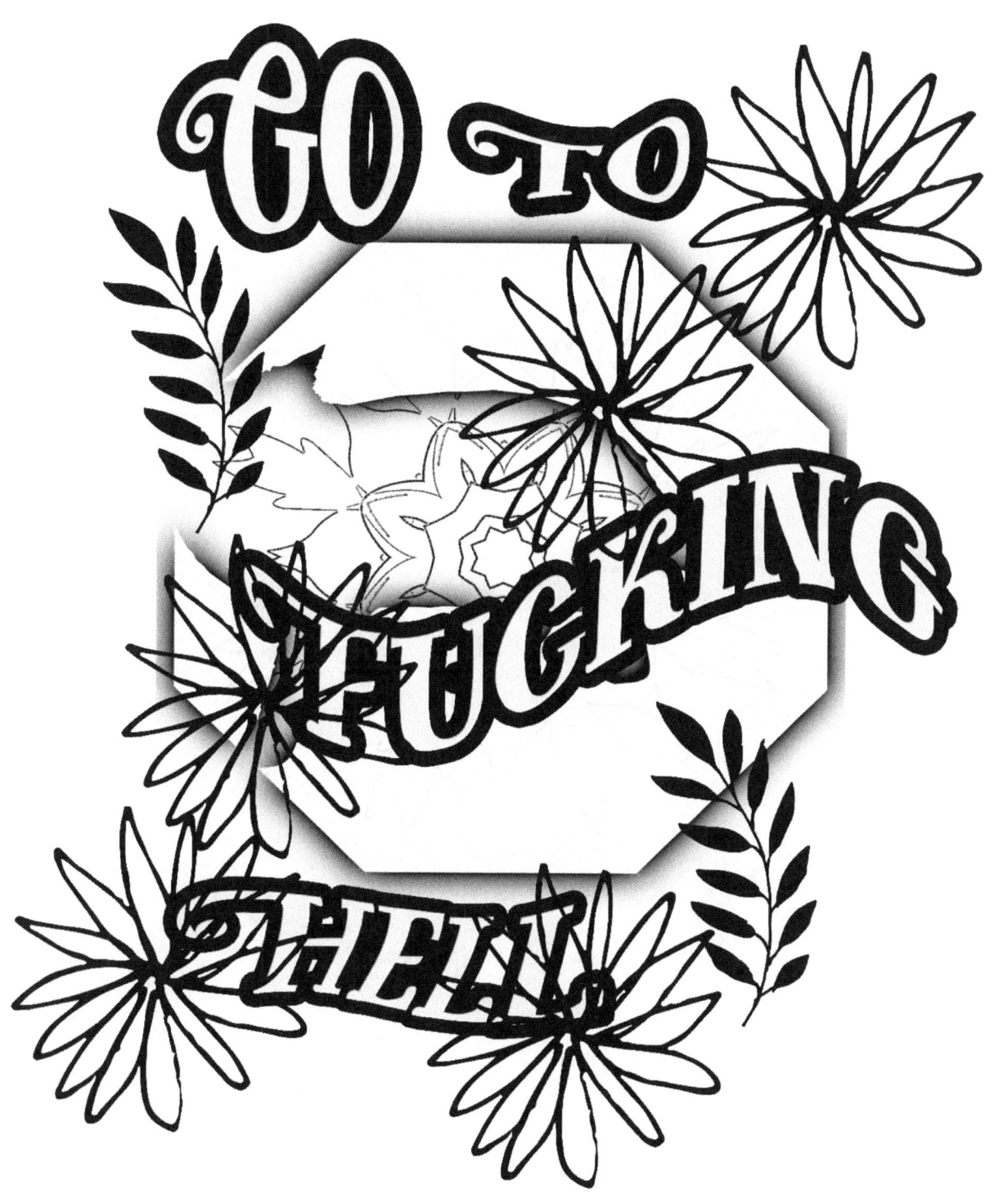

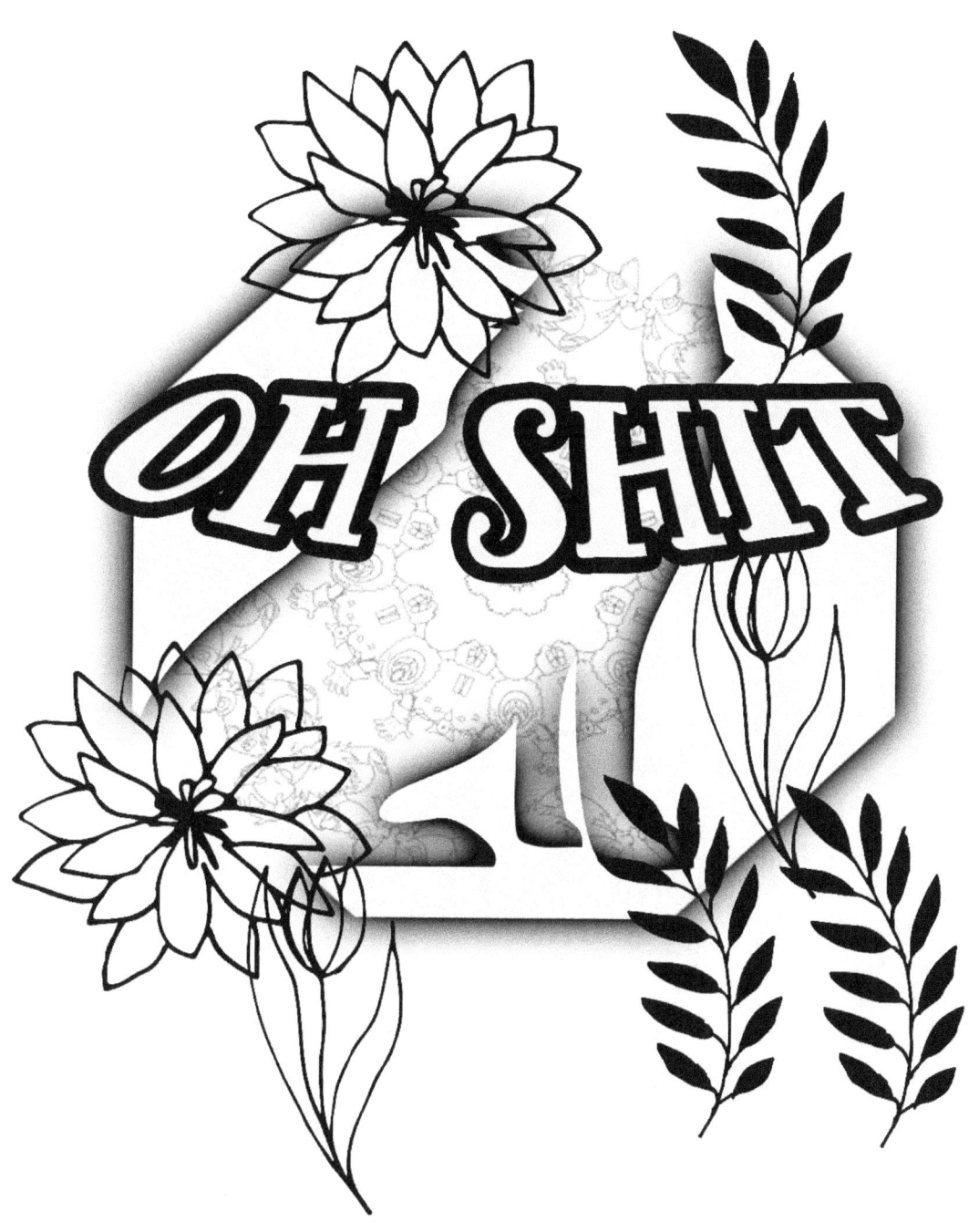

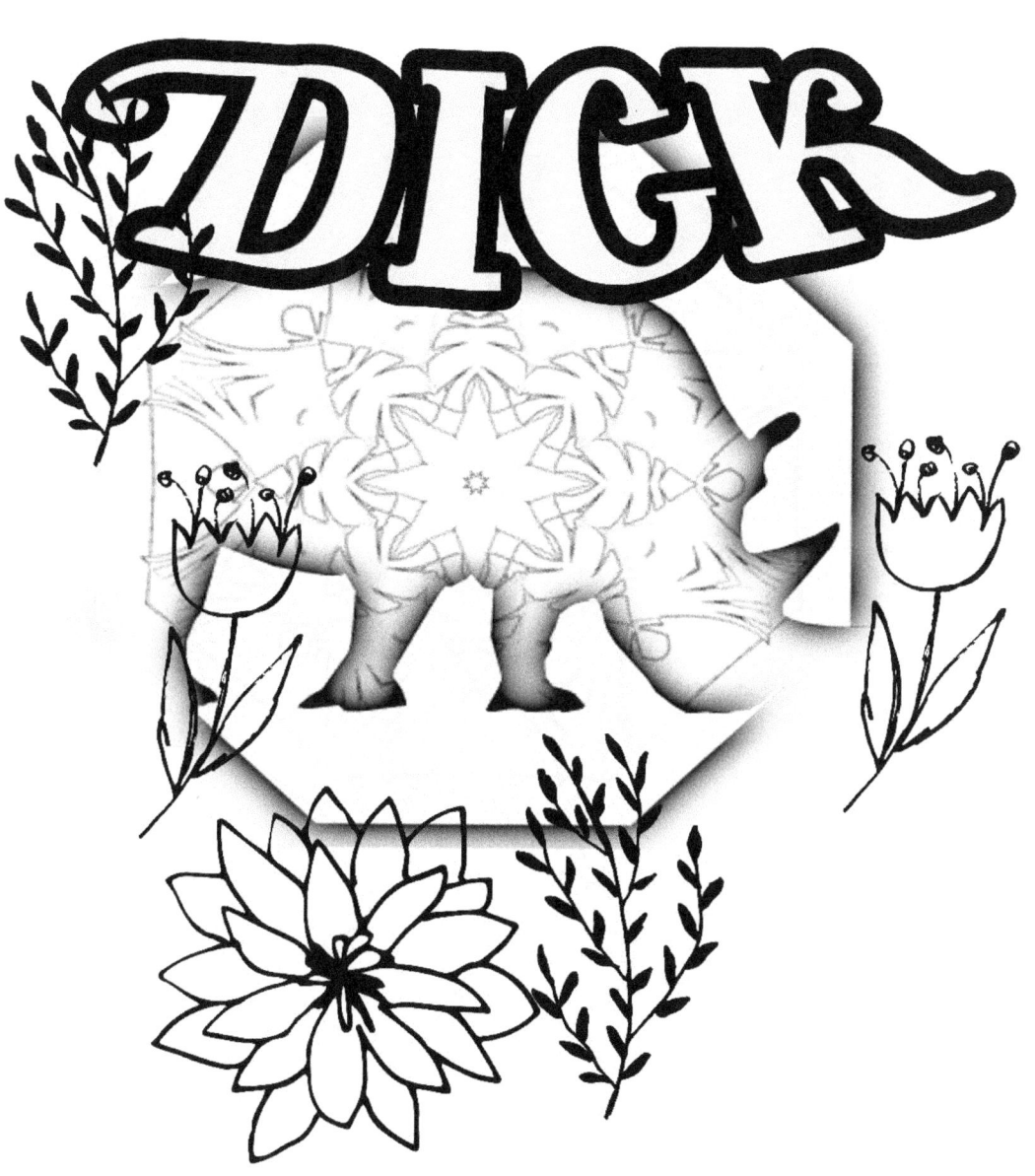

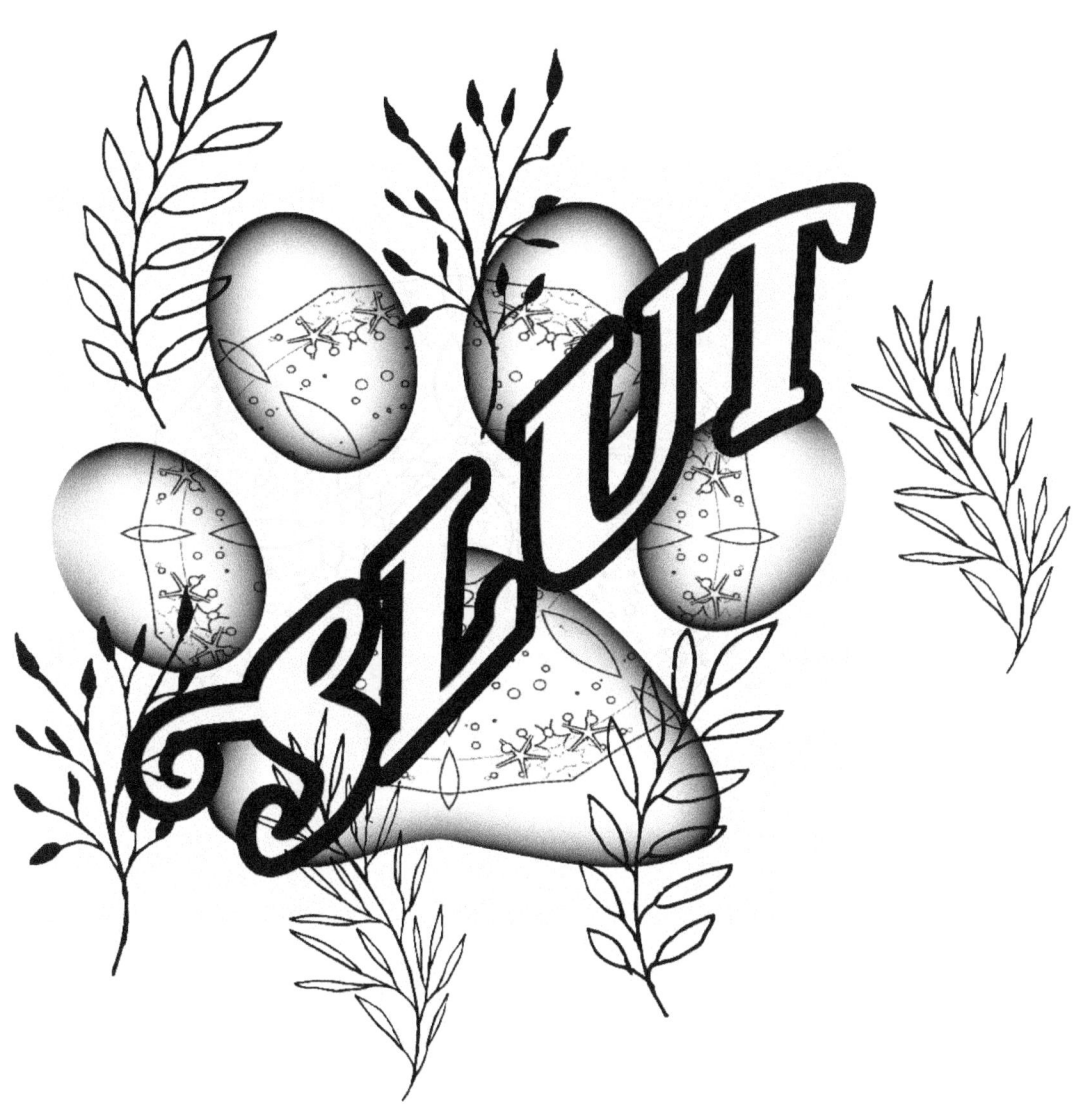

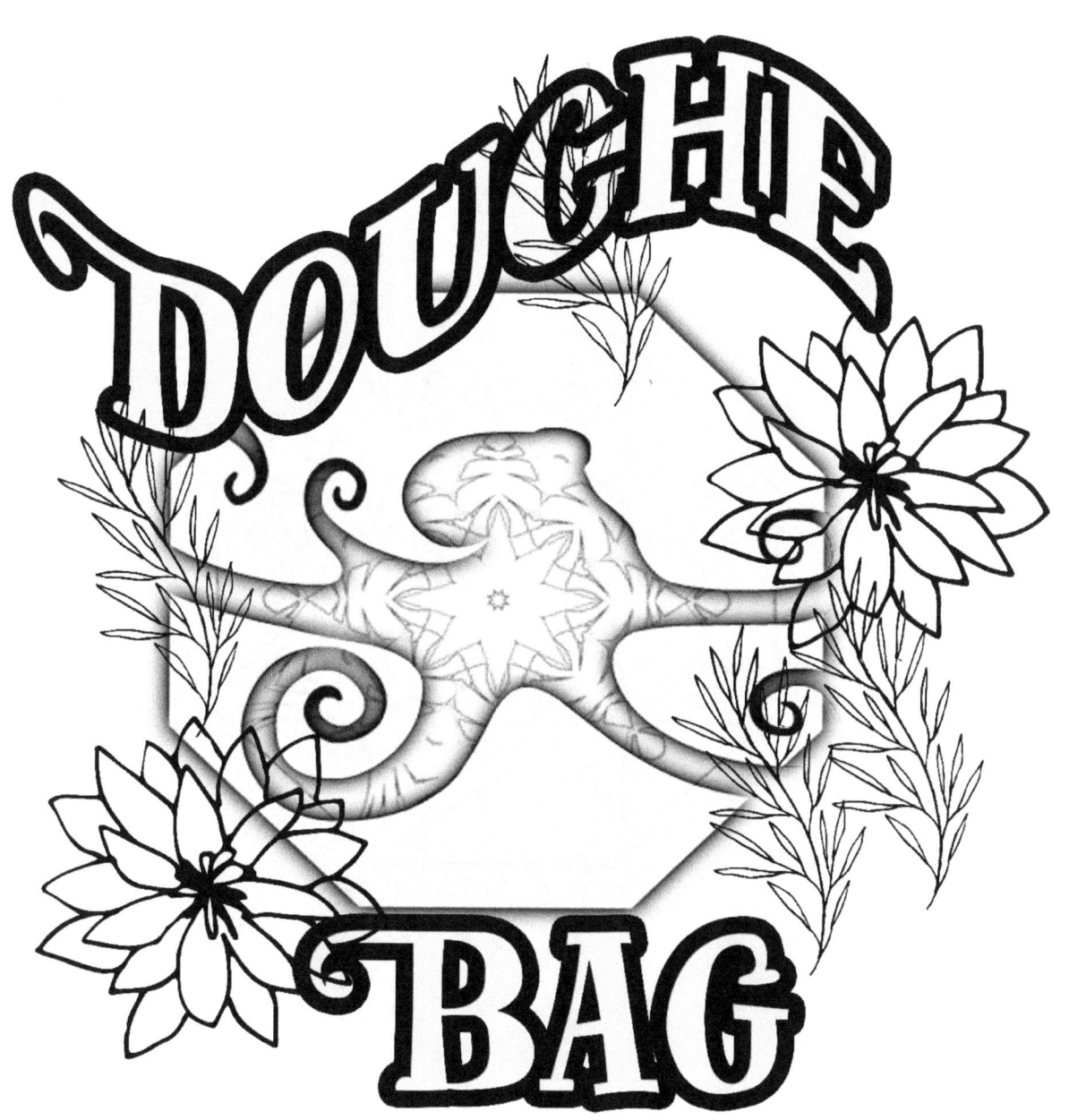

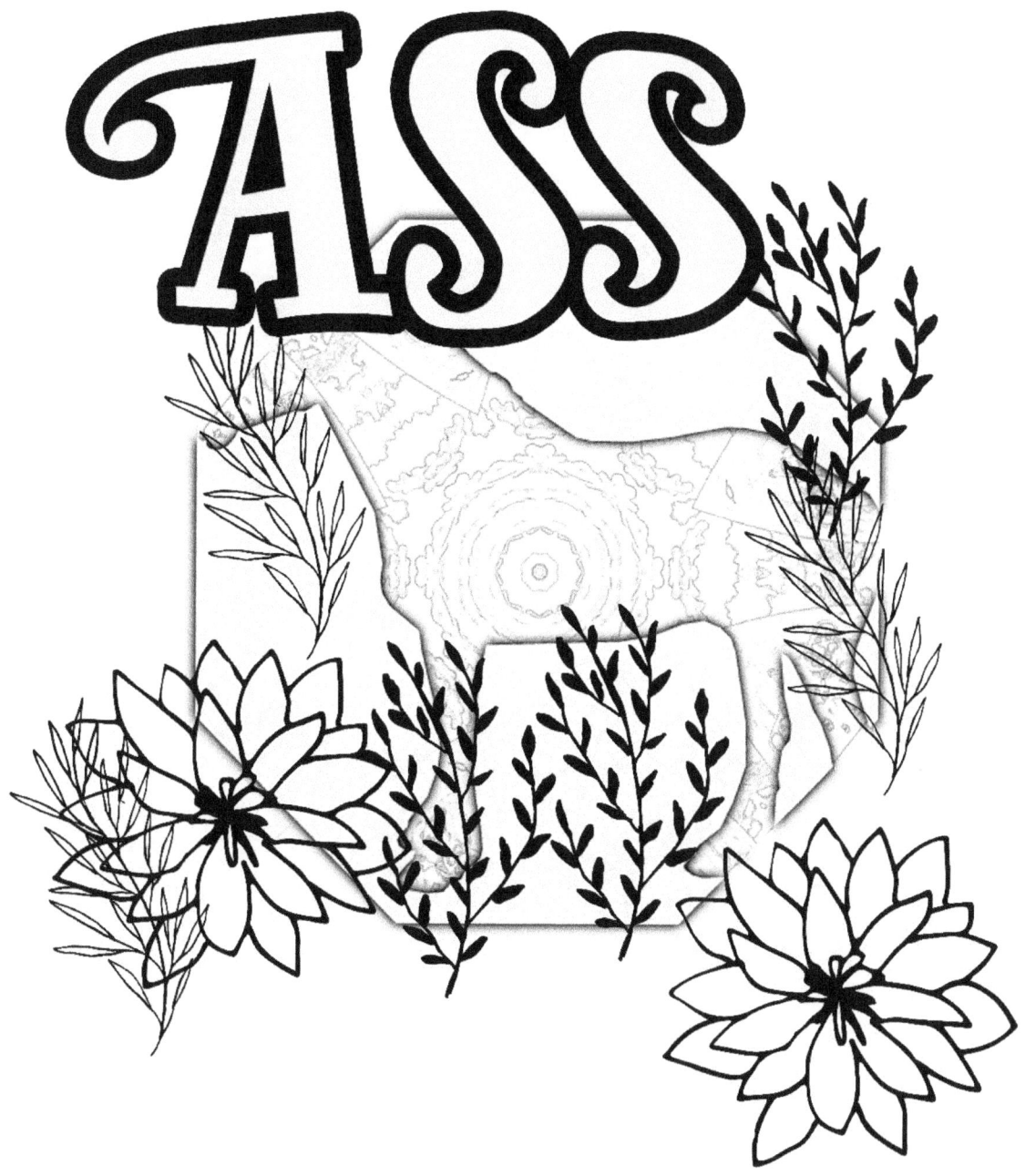

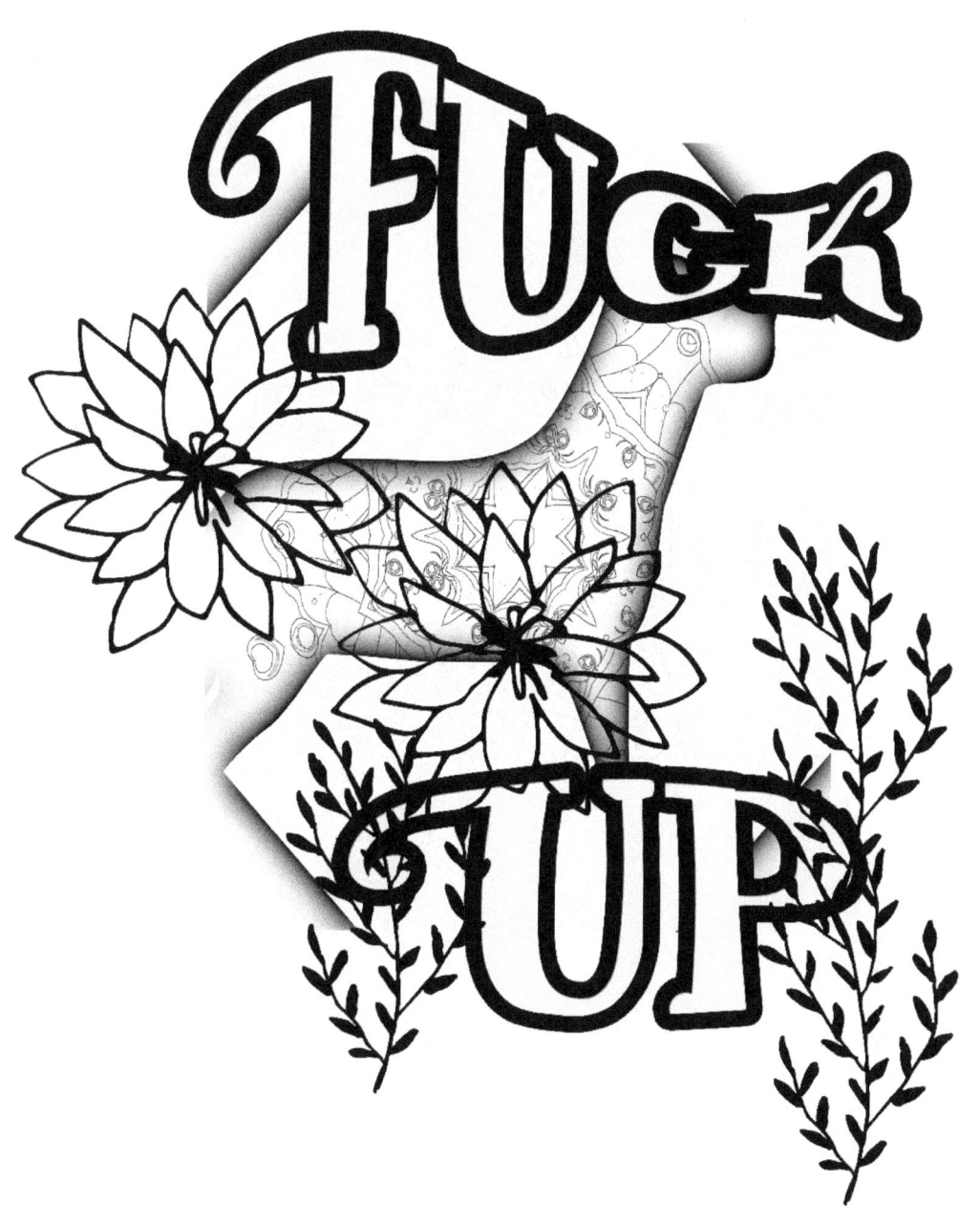

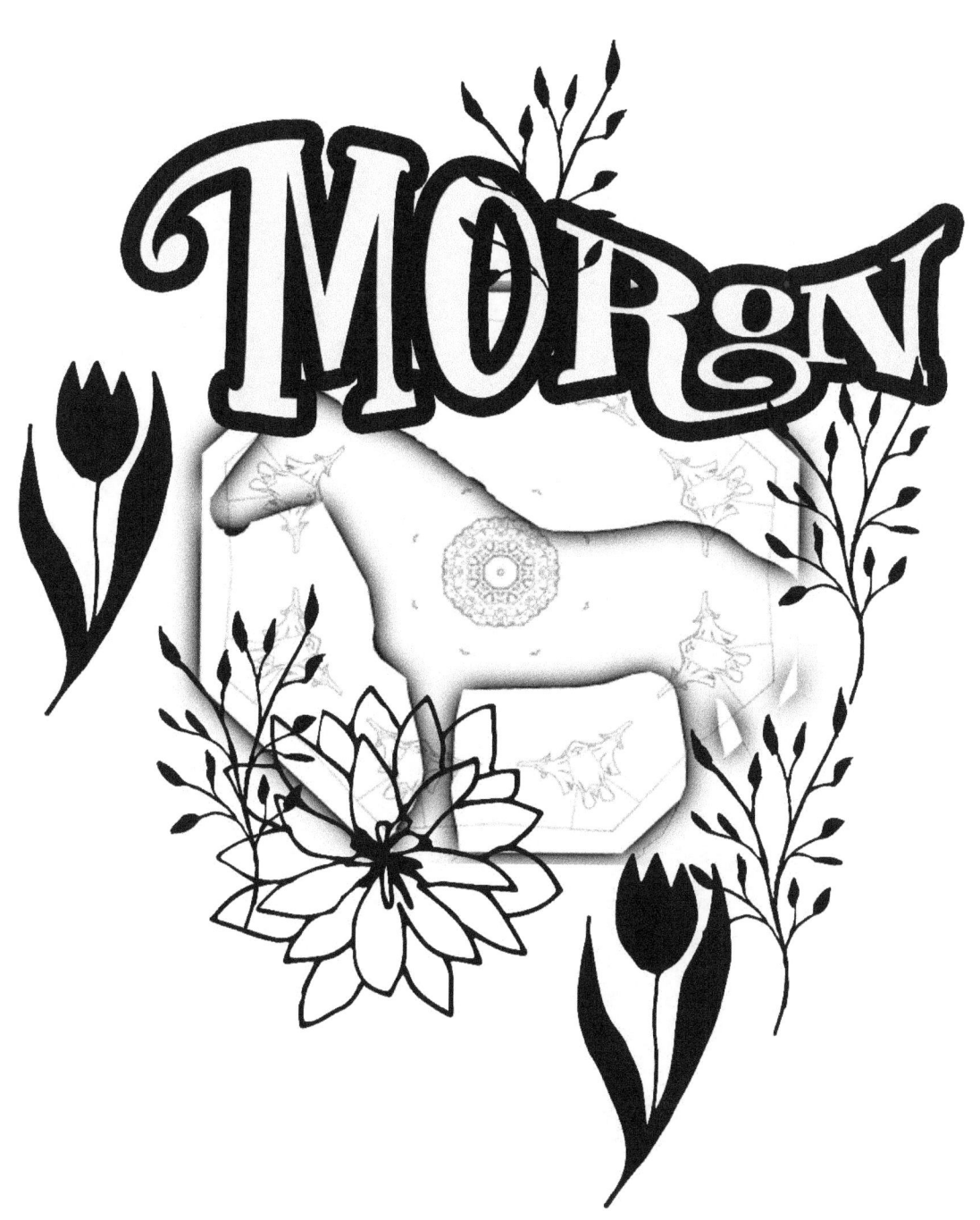

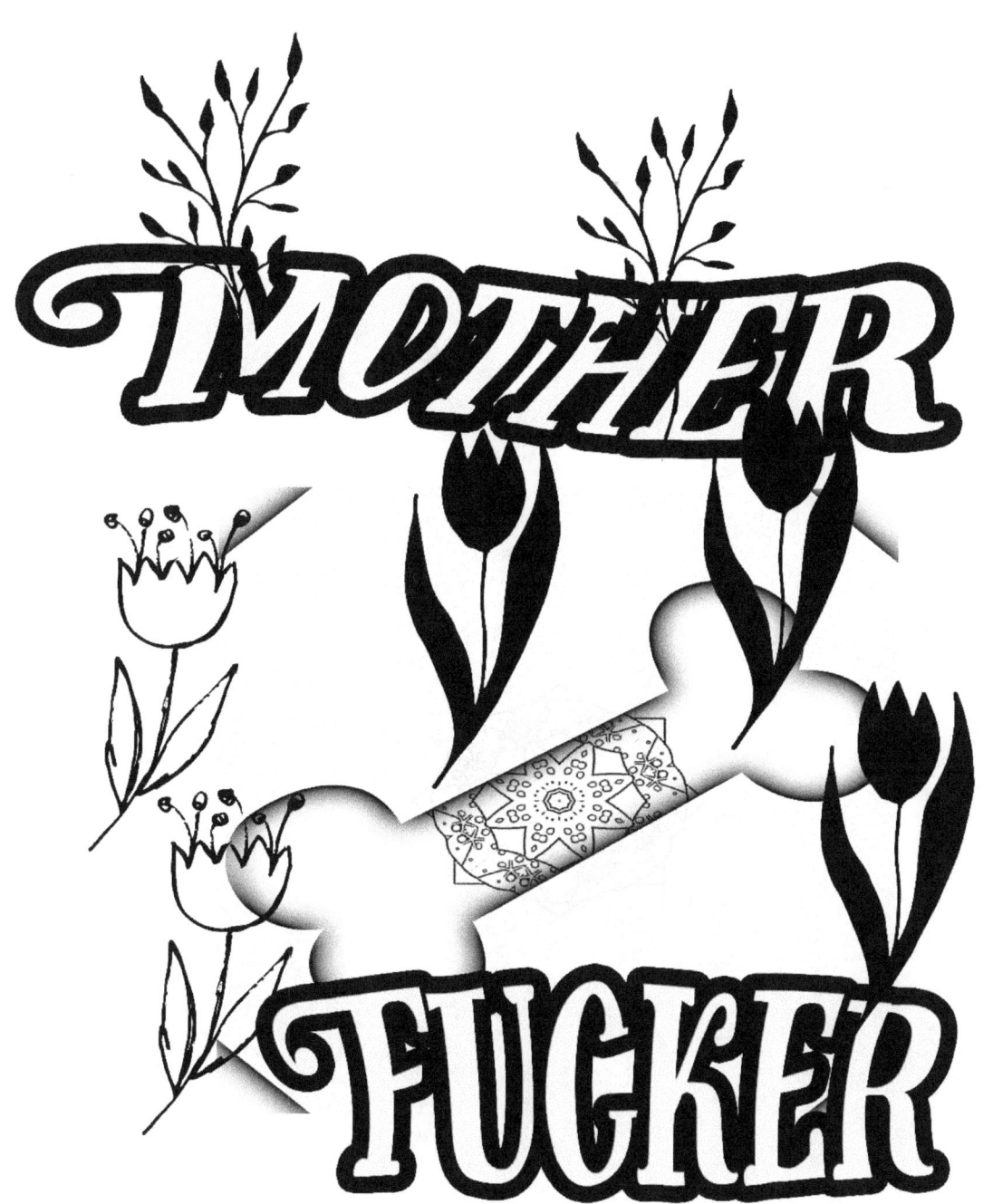

Note

www.ingramcontent.com/pod-product-compliance
Lightning Source LLC
Chambersburg PA
CBHW080643190526
45169CB00009B/3478